IMAGES
of England

BEXHILL-ON-SEA

THE SECOND SELECTION

BEXHILL
ON - SEA

IMAGES
of England

BEXHILL-ON-SEA
THE SECOND SELECTION

Julian Porter

TEMPUS

Sackville Road, *c.* 1910. Sackville is the surname of the Earls De La Warr. In the distance is the bridge, known as the Sackville Arch, where the railway line crosses the road. This was one of the original cattle arches made when the line was built in 1846, it was widened in 1892 to allow for the increased traffic of the new resort.

Frontispiece: Miss Bexhill 1934, shown here appearing as the Queen of Hearts in the Christmas pantomime at the Lyceum Theatre, London.

First published 2002
Copyright © Julian Porter, 2002

Tempus Publishing Limited
The Mill, Brimscombe Port,
Stroud, Gloucestershire, GL5 2QG

ISBN 0 7524 2627 3

Typesetting and origination by
Tempus Publishing Limited
Printed in Great Britain by
Midway Colour Print, Wiltshire

Contents

The De La Warr Pavilion from the east, 1936. In the foreground is the model boating pond and to the left is 22 Marina Court Avenue where, in 1911, the Maharajah of Cooch Behar died. Behind the Pavilion is the Metropole Hotel.

Acknowledgements

I would like to thank the following for their help and use of their photographs: Emma Tickner, Don Phillips, Peter Fairhurst, Ann Vollor, Margaret Rymer, Gordon Edwards, Mr Freeman, Mr Heather, Mr Randall, David Hughes, Elma Bates, the volunteers and committee of Bexhill Museum and Bexhill Costume Museum.

Bibliography

The Bexhill Almanack & Directory: various issues
Fairley, Alastair *Bucking the Trend*: The Pavilion Trust (Bexhill) 2001
Gray, F. ed. *Bexhill Voices* CCE University of Sussex (Falmer) 1994
Green, H. & Pinney, A. *Britain in Old Photographs Bexhill-on-Sea*: Alan Sutton 1989
Guilmant, Aylwin ed. *Bexhill Voices Two*: Bexhill Voices Two (Bexhill) 1999
Guilmant, Aylwin *Bexhill-on-Sea: A Pictorial History*: Phillimore (Chichester) 1982
L.J. Bartley *The Story of Bexhill*: F.J. Parsons Ltd. (Bexhill-on-Sea) 1971
Mullens, W.H. *A Short History of Bexhill* (Bexhill) 1927
Porter, J. *Annie Lady Brassey* (Bexhill) 1996
Porter, J. *Images of England, Bexhill-on-Sea*: Tempus (Stroud) 1998

Foreword

I am delighted to have been asked to write a few words in support of the tireless work done by Julian Porter, the Rother District Curator; in this second book of photographs - he has certainly captured the atmosphere and many of the sights of Bexhill over the last century. Bexhill Museum was established in 1914 and has, over the years, built up an impressive collection of objects, documents and a great number of photographs, from which Julian's carefully chosen selection is reproduced in these pages.

The Museum is a fascinating place with exhibits covering Bexhill over many centuries. There is information about the huge number of independent boarding schools that were established in Bexhill during the early twentieth century, and had an unusual effect on the development of the town. Many of the parents were working abroad and objects from throughout the British Empire and beyond were brought back to the town, many eventually ending up in Bexhill Museum.

Today Bexhill's built environment shows a mixture of old and new features. Redevelopment and wartime bombing have taken their toll but the town centre is still largely, despite the trappings of modern life, as it appeared when built in the late 1890s and early years of the twentieth century.

In 2002 we are celebrating the 100th anniversary of Bexhill as an Incorporated Borough, when the town's local government came of age and was able to elect its own mayor. Famously in 1902 the first motorcar races were held on the seafront, also three new railway stations and a branch line opened, making the journey time to London half an hour quicker than it is today. Considerable extra resources have been made available to the town and it is hoped that some of the sense of optimism and civic pride that characterized the events of 1902 can be recaptured now, one hundred years later.

Councillor Peter Fairhurst. B.Ed.(hons)
Mayor of Bexhill 2002-2003

Introduction

This is the second selection of old photographs from the archives of Bexhill Museum, and it again offers the opportunity to explore the town's fascinating past. This selection also gives us the chance to look at some more unusual images that had to be left out of the first book.

Now to briefly sum up Bexhill's past. The first mention of Bexhill was in a charter of King Offa in 772, he founded a church here and gave it and the land to Bishop Oswald of Selsey. The Bishops later moved their base to Chichester and they were the main landowner until 1570 when Queen Elizabeth I gave Bexhill to Sir Thomas Sackville - his descendents the Dukes of Dorset held Bexhill until the mid-nineteenth century. Through marriage the land passed to the Earls De La Warr and it was the 7th Earl who in 1883 had the first seawall built and the fashionable new resort of Bexhill-on-Sea constructed. The 8th Earl De La Warr carried on his father's work, possibly with more enthusiasm than good sense, and put the town on the map by hosting Britain's first motorcar races on his private seafront road in 1902. During the First World War a military camp was established at Cooden Camp where the Southdowns Regiment was raised and troops from Canada and South Africa trained. The 9th Earl De La Warr is best known for inspiring and championing the building of the world famous De La Warr Pavilion, our 'People's Palace'. In the Second World War Bexhill seemed likely to become the front line of an expected invasion and had a strong military presence. Post war the local economy declined, many of the schools did not return to Bexhill and those that did gradually closed or moved away. The availability of cheap package holidays left the town unable to compete. The resort became more residential and amenities and hotels for holidaymakers closed down.

I must thank all those who have given old photographs of Bexhill to the Museum. They are the basis for most of our exhibitions and, of course, publications such as this. There are still many local events and locations of which we don't have any images, so please look through any old photographs you may have and come and see me at the Museum.

Julian Porter
Bexhill, June 2002

One
Bexhill Old Town

St Peter's church in 1896. The church has Saxon origins and may be the church mentioned in King Offa's AD 772 charter. The church was substantially modified in 1878, during this work the 'Bexhill Stone', a piece of decorative Saxon stonework was discovered beneath the nave. This drawing is signed F.H.H. although it is not known who this was.

St Peters church from the south-east, c. 1910. The nave is thought to be Saxon and the tower added after the Norman invasion of 1066. An eighteenth-century gallery, lit by dormer windows on the south side of the church was removed during the Victorian 'restorations' of 1878.

RE-OPENING OF BEXHILL PARISH CHURCH,
MARCH 2ND 1908,
THE LORD BISHOP OF CHICHESTER.

The Bishop of Chichester at St. Peter's church, 2 March 1908. Bishop Ridgeway visited for the reopening of the church after the extension of the north aisle, which gave seating for 250 more parishioners. For most of its history Bexhill belonged to the bishops of Chichester, King Offa had given it and the church to their predecessors, the bishops of Selsey in AD 772.

St Peter's church from Church Street, 1937. The lych-gates were built in the early 1920s, replacing the simple gates that can be seen in earlier photographs.

Bexhill Old Town viewed from the tower of St Peter's church, winter 1907. The gasworks in Ashdown Road can be seen at the top left and South Lodge at the top right.

Triumphal arch in Bexhill Old Town, 1900. The decorations were to welcome the 8th Earl De La Warr back to the Manor House after his return from the Boer War. Edwin Bunting, headmaster of St Peter's boys' school, designed the arch.

Jubilee Clock and walnut tree in 1900. The clock was built to commemorate Queen Victoria's Golden Jubilee in 1887. The walnut tree was originally in the corner of the Manor House grounds but rather than cutting it down when the road was widened it was kept as a roundabout and landmark for the Old Town.

Cutting down the walnut tree, 1906. Earl Brassey used some of the wood from the tree to make a gavel for the Town Hall.

The walnut tree stump, c. 1908. Despite being cut down in 1906 the stump was not removed until 1921. The Manor House is in the background.

Bexhill Manor House, c. 1895. The south elevation after the restoration for Viscount and Lady Cantelupe in 1892, following their wedding in 1891. During this work the Manor House became the first home in Bexhill to have a telephone. In 1896 the Viscount became 8th Earl De La Warr. Muriel, Countess De La Warr, divorced the Earl in 1902 and moved back with her father, Earl Brassey, at Normanhurst Court, Catsfield.

Bexhill Manor House, c. 1917, the east elevation. The Manor House was lived in by the Du Mont family from 1903 until 1912. In 1919 the Manor House was bought by Sir Robert Leicester Harmsworth, his family lived there until 1963, it was demolished in 1968.

Bexhill Old Town 1921. This photograph was taken shortly before the stump of the walnut tree was removed in 1921. On the left is the north side of the Manor House.

Hastings Road, c. 1923. The Manor House, now an ornamental ruin, is on the right. One of the reasons why the Manor House was demolished was to widen the road. Parts of the Manor House were dated to the thirteenth century; it was probably built about 1250, making it the second oldest building in Bexhill, after the church.

Countess De La Warr with her daughters Myra and Avice at Bexhill Manor House, c. 1898. Myra Idina, the eldest daughter, was born in February 1893 and Avice Ela Muriel in July 1897.

The 8th Earl De La Warr and family in 1900. Countess De La Warr was Muriel Brassey, daughter of Earl Brassey and the famous Victorian writer, traveller and collector Annie Lady Brassey. This photograph was taken in the grounds of the Brassey's Normanhurst estate, Catsfield, shortly after the birth of Herbrand, the future 9th Earl De La Warr.

Bexhill High Street, c. 1920. The Little Beehive shop, formerly Hibberd's chemist shop, is on the left and next to it is Pocock's butchers shop. Pocock's was the oldest surviving shop in Bexhill; it was opened in 1801 but was closed in 1998. In the distance South Lodge, one of the buildings in the Manor House grounds can be seen at the end of the High Street.

Chantry Lane, 10 March 1925. A bus is starting to descend into the sunken lane, on the left is Barrack Hall and on the right Chantry Cottage. Barrack Hall stood at the eastern end of the barracks that were established in 1798 although it remained a private residence. The King's German Legion, Hanoverian troops who became part of the British army to help defeat Napoleon, was based at the barracks between 1804 and 1814. Chantry Cottage was home to Alex Sanders, the self-styled 'King of the Witches', from 1973 to 1986.

The Metropolitan Convalescent Home dining room, c. 1920. The convalescent home was opened in 1881, at first it was mixed but another home, of very similar design, was opened at Cooden in 1905 for men and the Old Town home then only received women. It was demolished in 1988.

The Metropolitan Convalescent Home sitting room, c. 1934. The home's size and position on the brow of the hill made it a major landmark on the skyline. The Convalescent Home actually pre-dated the development of the resort, which did not start until 1883.

Bexhill Hospital, 1933. Princess Helena Victoria, a cousin of King George V, opened the Hospital in May 1933. Also in attendance was the 9th Earl De La Warr, during his mayoralty, and deputy mayor Mrs Meads.

Belle Hill, 19 August 1951. *The Daily Express* Tour of Britain bicycle race. On the right is Warburton's corn merchants and grain-mill, which opened on the site in 1887 and was demolished in 1976. Warburton's also opened a shop in Town Hall Square in 1910. Much of historic Belle Hill was destroyed by the construction of the Old Town bypass in 1978. The bypass opened in 1980 and was renamed King Offa Way.

Bexhill Steam Laundry, Belle Hill, 1900. The procession taking the 8th Earl to the Town Hall in triumph after his return from the Boer War, passing the Steam Laundry.

Bexhill Laundry, Belle Hill, 1928. Here hampers of laundry are being readied to go back to their respective establishments. Given the large number of hotels and boarding schools in Bexhill at this time, the laundry was a very important place.

Cockett's grocers shop, Belle Hill, *c.* 1890. Cockett's shop was later moved to London Road.

The Queen's Head, Belle Hill, *c.* 1960. Formerly the Black Horse, it closed in 1977 and was demolished as part of the construction of King Offa Way. Sophia Braizer, the daughter of the innkeeper, brought a paternity suit against an officer of the King's German Legion in 1813 and was successful. Bexhill's first drill hall was built behind the Queen's Head, although access was from London Road.

De La Warr Road, *c.* 1910. The open area on the right was the Bexhill Golf Course; it has now been completely covered by housing. Perhaps the greatest difference between this view and the current situation is the amount of traffic. De La Warr Road is the main route from Bexhill to Hastings and is exceedingly busy.

Jubilee beacon bonfire, Hastings Road, 1887. This thirty-five foot high bonfire was lit to commemorate Queen Victoria's Jubilee on 19 June and did not go out until the 22 June. At the base of the bonfire are Councillor W. J. Smith, Mr Ney, who built the bonfire, and Mr Burton.

Two
Seafront

Natural cast of a dinosaur footprint from Bexhill beach. The local geology is exceptional, being the remains of a low-lying freshwater landscape of 130 million years ago. Dinosaur fossils are not uncommon but perhaps the most spectacular are their preserved footprints that are sometimes uncovered on the foreshore. This specimen is probably from a carnivorous dinosaur such as *Megalosaurus*.

The Sackville Hotel and Tropical Garden on De La Warr Parade, c. 1896. The 7th Earl De La Warr developed the small agricultural village of Bexhill into the fashionable resort of Bexhill-on-Sea. Work began with the building of the seawall by John Webb in 1883. The Sackville Hotel was opened on 23 July 1890 by the 7th Earl De La Warr and the eastern half was at first retained as a family residence, Sackville House.

The 8th Earl De La Warr, c. 1898. Viscount Cantelupe became Earl when his father died in 1896. He was born in 1869 and was only 27 when he became Earl. He married Muriel Brassey in 1891 at which time his father gave him responsibility for managing his Bexhill estate. The enthusiastic, ambitious and inexperienced 8th Earl was the driving force behind the resort in its early years.

Hotel Riposo, De La Warr Parade, c. 1920. The Riposo was built, slightly to the east of the Sackville Hotel, in 1901. It was eventually demolished in 1961 and Cavendish Court was built on the site.

The De La Warr Gates, c. 1895. In 1895 the 8th Earl attempted to sell East Parade to the Bexhill Urban District Council, but they would not pay the amount the Earl wanted. Instead the Earl decided to manage his portion of the seafront, rather than his original plan to develop and sell. The East Parade was re-branded as De La Warr Parade and the De La Warr Gates at the western end to show the Earl's personal involvement. The Bexhill Corporation finally bought De La Warr Parade in 1913 at which time the gates were taken down.

The Cycle Chalet and Sackville Hotel 1900. The Chalet was part of the Bicycle Boulevard that was opened in 1896 on De La Warr Parade. The 8th Earl was at that time chairman of Dunlop, a connection that later developed into an interest in motorcars. The decorations may be for the Earl's return from the Boer War in 1900.

The motorcar racetrack on De La Warr Parade, 1902. The 8th Earl hosted Britain's first motorcar races on his Bexhill estate on 19 May 1902. The Automobile Club of Great Britain and Ireland organized the event and it attracted competitors from Europe. The inserted image shows the De La Warr Gates and the Kursaal.

The 1902 races. The Sackville Hotel, on the right, was used as the Automobile Club's headquarters during the event. Thousands of spectators watched the races and the event was covered by the international press. Inserted is a photograph of Baron Henri de Rothchild's 40hp Mercedes.

Leon Serpollet's steam car, the *Easter Egg*, 1902. This car won the races in 1902 achieving a speed of just over fifty-four miles an hour. In 2002 a working replica of this remarkable vehicle took part in the Centenary Bexhill 100 Festival of Motoring event.

Crowds inspect the cars taking part in the Motor Reliability Trials, 6 September 1902. There were going to be more races in May but a High Court injunction by a Mr Mayner stopped the later events, as he claimed they blocked access to his seafront properties. Just visible in the background is a caravan that belonged to Dr Gordon Stables who visited Bexhill in 1902 and helped publicise the town.

The 1904 motorcar races. The Earl, despite the injunction against seafront races, held races again in 1904. Unlike the 1902 races that had a flying start from the top of Galley Hill, the 1904 event raced in the opposite direction. Further speed trials were held in 1905 and 1906 but Bexhill was unable to compete with the opening of the racing circuit at Brooklands in 1907.

Decorated car at the 1904 races. This is Mrs Harvey Du Cros's entry in the decorated car competition. Female motorists took part in both the 1902 and 1904 events. The vehicles used were not exclusively petrol driven – steam cars were popular and, in the case of Leon Serpollet's *Easter Egg*, faster, and there were also several electrically powered cars.

Bexhill *Concours d'Élégance*, De La Warr Parade 1935. These car shows began in 1934, and in 1936 the Concours was held on the terrace of the newly opened De La Warr Pavilion. In 1954 a commemorative motorcar rally was held on the seafront and in 1990 there was the first Bexhill 100 Festival of Motoring.

Bexhill Horse Show on De La Warr Parade, 27 May 1912. The first horse show was in 1903, the event started on the seafront and the participants then paraded around the town.

Exercise for children, De La Warr Parade, 1933. Keep fit was taken very seriously during the 1930s and was part of the 'Health and Holidays' ethos of Bexhill at that time.

Galley Hill, 1937. The area where the people are seated is now where the water treatment works are sited, at the foot of Galley Hill. Sackville Lodge, on the top of the hill, was built in 1903 and demolished in 1968, parts of the garden still survive.

The Kursaal, c. 1898. The Kursaal was an entertainment hall built on De La Warr Parade by the 8th Earl De La Warr in 1896. It was intended to be a pier but only the landward section was ever built. It was demolished in 1936, just after the opening of the De La Warr Pavilion, and the sailing clubhouse now occupies the site.

The Kursaal garden, c. 1912. The beach beside the Kursaal is high and rarely covered by the sea; this area was laid out as a garden with plants in tubs, tables and chairs. The Kursaal deck, here covered with awnings is in the background.

The Incorporation banquet at the Kursaal, 21 May 1902. This event marked an eventful day in the history of the town and was the culmination of work that began in 1898, to make Bexhill into an incorporated borough. Bexhill was the last Sussex town to be incorporated and it was the first royal charter to be granted by King Edward VII. The Bexhill Borough Council was formed, which had greater powers than the previous Urban District Council, and also gave Bexhill its first mayor.

The Kursaal Deck, c. 1900. In 1899 a tea lounge and deck were built on the eastern side of the Kursaal. This created an open air seating area, which in part made up for the building not being completed as a pier. The deck could be covered with awnings when required.

The Kursaal and De La Warr Gates, c. 1911. The 'crocodile' of schoolchildren in the foreground would have been a familiar sight in Bexhill during the first half of the twentieth century as the town was saturated with independent schools. The De La Warr gates were taken down in 1913.

The Kursaal, c. 1935. The Kursaal is shown here right at the end of its life, it was demolished in 1936. The roof was altered in 1925; this did little to improve the look of the building. In 1935 the beach on the western side was leased to The Dodgem Company as a leisure centre. The poster is advertising Philip Yorke's repertory company that performed at the Kursaal in its last years.

Floodlit flowerbeds on Central Parade, 1937. This is the area north of Marina Arcade; the War Memorial can just be seen in the background.

Central Parade, c. 1905. On the left is Marina Arcade, then Marina Court (1901-1970), Roberts Marine Mansions (1895-1954) and right, Wilton Court, which was built in 1900.

Central Parade, 1962. This shows a curious mixture of old and new features; Marina Court, which was not demolished until 1970 is clearly visible on the left; Roberts Marine Mansions have gone and been replaced by Dalmore Court, built in 1961, and on the right Marina Garage is still present, the site is now occupied by a modern block of flats, rather confusingly also called Marina Court. On the far right, at the end of Marina Garage, part of Forte's Ice Cream Parlour can be seen.

Forte's Ice Cream Parlour, 1935. Built on the eastern end of Marina Garage, Forte's was the place to go for the younger inhabitants of Bexhill from the '30s to the '50s. Forte's closed in 1973.

Central Parade looking west, 1934. The Kursaal is seen here with its higher roof, added during extensive alterations in 1925. Although I always refer to the building as the Kursaal its name was changed to the Pavilion in 1915 due to anti-German feelings created by the First World War. Near to the Kursaal is the War Memorial that was unveiled on 12 December 1920.

Sea Angling Club, c. 1914. This is the eastern end of Marina Arcade and the occasion is the christening of Monica Sheffield. The East Sussex branch of the British Sea Anglers Society was founded in Bexhill in 1893, this eventually closed and the Bexhill Sea Angling Association started in 1914. The Association stopped during the Second World War and reopened in 1954.

Farmerie Tea Rooms c. 1910. Situated on the north-eastern corner of Marina Arcade, it was replaced by the Green Tea Room. To the right of the picture is part of the Cairo Toy and Fancy Repository. Marina Arcade was built in 1901 for Mr Durward-Brown by The Martin Wells Company; they also built the Granville Hotel in 1901-1902.

Green Tea Room, Marine Arcade, 1935. This rare interior shot shows the Green Tea Room, successor to the Farmerie Tea Rooms that opened in 1901. The Arcade was designed in a 'Moorish style' to accommodate a 375 foot long swimming pool with facilities for 500 spectators, this idea was never implemented.

Channel View c. 1926. Channel View is the seaward side of Marina Arcade and was built in 1901. There were plans to build a pier from this site and the street plans show the roads at either end as Pier View East and Pier View West. The block of bungalows next to the De La Warr Pavilion on Marina Court Avenue were built between 1902 and 1908.

Marina Court, c. 1970. Seen here from the steps at the end of Marina Arcade this block of apartments, with shops at street level, was opened in 1901 and demolished in 1970. The site is now the eastern end of the De La Warr Pavilion car park. The land was originally known as the 'Triangular Plot' and was owned by Earl De La Warr. It is said that he let the rest of the town use it as a public open space on condition that they maintained it, but in 1895 he took it back, because the Urban District Council were not looking after it, and sold it to Mr Gold who built Marina Court. The 8th Earl rented an apartment there in 1902 when he was estranged from Countess De La Warr.

Coastguard Cottages, c. 1894. An early view looking towards the Coastguard Cottages that once stood on the site now occupied by the De La Warr Pavilion. The low grassy cliff, on which the Colonnade was built in 1911, was known as The Horn. On the left is a building, probably The Marine Hotel – later Roberts Marine Mansions, under construction. The provision for swimming appears quite limited with one bathing machine and ticket huts.

Model boating pond, Marina, 1937. Between the Coastguard Cottages, where the De La Warr Pavilion now stands, and Marina Court was an ornamental garden and model boating pond. The garden was eventually sacrificed in order to extend the car park.

Bathing machines, The Horn, *c.* 1895. The Rowing Clubhouse is just visible in the distance. Bathing machines allowed female swimmers to change and swim in private, they are only a feature of the earliest photographs of the resort because they were soon superseded by the bathing stations associated with mixed bathing.

The Colonnade, *c.* 1911. The
Colonnade was made to
commemorate King George V's
coronation in 1911. It was built into
a low sandy cliff known as The Horn,
just below the Coastguard Cottages.
The site was developed and renamed
Central Parade in 1910 and a
makeshift bandstand set up. The
Colonnade became a less exclusive
alternative to the 8th Earl's Kursaal.

Work on the beach below the
Colonnade, 24 January 1929. The
Colonnade used to extend further
out over the beach than it does
today, an outer walkway allowed
people to walk along the promenade
while the Colonnade was closed off
during a performance. In the
background is the Metropole Hotel.

Highland pipers and dancers at the Colonnade, August 1912. The bandstand, now lost, is clearly shown, as is a temporary stage set up for dancing. Bands were the preferred form of entertainment in the early resort and would have made the seafront a much noisier place than we are used to today.

The *Daily Mirror* 8 performing at the Colonnade, c. 1934. The troupe appeared in Bexhill a number of times in the mid 1930s, entertaining the crowds with their keep-fit routines.

Bathing Belles at the Colonnade, 1935. Events and competitions of all kinds were organized for the entertainment of the visitors and residents.

Roberts Marine Mansions, c. 1910. The photographer is probably at one of the windows of Marina Court, the road on the left is Devonshire Road and Marina is on the right. Built as the Marine Hotel in 1895 it was bought by John Reynolds Roberts, a successful London draper, as a holiday home for the trade and renamed Roberts Marine Mansions. It was bombed during the Second World War and demolished in 1954. Dalmore Court was built on the site in 1961.

The Metropole Hotel, *c.* 1899. Building work on the hotel began in 1897 and it opened for business in May 1900. The Metropole was second only to the Sackville Hotel and was visually more imposing due to its unique seafront location. The building was orientated to face west rather than south. During the Second World War the Metropole was a billet for the RAF, who in 1940 set fire to it, it was also bombed in 1941. The building was demolished in 1955 and the land used as a miniature golf course.

Beach Towers boarding house, *c.* 1910. Taken from the Metropole Hotel and looking west. Only the north-west tower, not seen here, still survives. The impressive terrace on the left is Marine Crescent, this run of houses was never completed and the street name was dropped by 1927. When constructed Marine Crescent was not considered to be part of West Parade.

Sea-bathing on West Parade, c. 1923. The ornate house, Oceania, is in the background, it was built in 1903. Even by this late date West Parade is relatively undeveloped.

Open air Sunday school on West Parade, c. 1968. There is an area of grass surrounded by a low wall just to the west of the miniature golf course. This was for many years used for open air Sunday schools and was referred to as the 'religious lawn'.

The Clock Tower on West Parade, c. 1905. The Clock Tower was supposed to commemorate the coronation of King Edward VII in 1902 but the whole project was dogged with problems, resulting in the work not being completed until 1904, much to the embarrassment of all concerned.

West Parade looking east, 1937. A busy scene on the seafront, in the background is the Metropole Hotel. Note the high ornamental bank separating the promenade from the road.

Donkey rides on West Parade, *c.* 1955. Many of the traditional forms of seaside entertainment seem to have been lacking in the early resort, this was in part due to a rather snobbish attitude towards what was seen as 'down-market' attractions. This photograph, at the far end of West Parade, shows that donkey rides at least were available.

Graham White's seaplane, 2 August 1912. *Wake Up England* was a Henri Farman biplane in which the pioneer aviator toured English resorts during the summer of 1912, sponsored by the *Daily Mail*. The first aeroplane to visit Bexhill was a Caudron biplane piloted by a Monsieur Duval in July 1911. He had been competing in a European Aviation Circuit race between London and Paris and had been forced to land at South Cliff.

Whale washed ashore between Pevensey Bay and the Sluice, 16 November 1864. This somewhat surreal image shows the skeleton of a whale washed ashore somewhere near Normans Bay. Clearly it has become an early tourist attraction.

Whale on Bexhill beach, 25 January 1938. This Bottle-nosed whale was washed ashore on 21 January 1938. Henry Sargent, curator of the Museum, is inspecting the whale. The skeleton is preserved in the stores of Bexhill Museum.

Whale washed ashore on Bexhill beach, November 1984. This was the last whale to come ashore, none of these whales beached alive but had died at sea and their bodies washed up. This specimen was buried in Pebsham tip but some of the ribs were later recovered and are displayed in the Museum.

Beach cabin life, c. 1905. This is a bathing station off De La Warr Parade; the crows-nest of The Sackville Hotel is just visible above the beach huts. Bexhill is reputed to be the first resort to permit mixed bathing, the date usually cited is 1901, but research has not revealed any changes to the by-laws to that effect at that time. There seems to have been mixed bathing in Bexhill before 1901, but Cromer is recorded as allowing mixed bathing since 1898, so it is unresolved who holds the title of 'birthplace of mixed bathing'.

Rock pool, 1925. These seaweed and barnacle encrusted rocks are exposed as a series of reefs along the beach. The rocks are about 130 million years old and contain a range of fossils from the Lower Cretaceous period.

The Sands, c. 1929. The builders of this sandcastle seem very pleased with themselves. Although the foreshore is entirely shingle there are extensive areas of sand, and admittedly mud, uncovered at low water.

50

Beach cricket, c. 1930. The beach provides recreational opportunities at low water. Horse riding on the beach was an early feature of the resort as well as more impromptu sporting events such as this.

Boating, c. 1936. Bexhill was an agricultural village prior to the development of the resort in 1883 and so never possessed a fishing fleet. The boats that can be seen in the early photographs are all pleasure craft.

Sunbathing, *c.* 1936. Bexhill's coat-of-arms, which was granted in 1907, has the motto *Sol et Salubritas,* which loosely translates as 'Sun and Health'.

De La Warr Pavilion dancing girls, off duty 1961. It is thought that the girls were part of the Starlight Rendezvous troupe that performed at the Pavilion during the 1960s.

Three
Street Scenes

The Town Hall decorated for Queen Elizabeth II's coronation in 1953. On the left is the extension to the Town Hall that was opened by Baron Buckhurst, the future 9th Earl De La Warr, in 1908.

The Lane Memorial in Town Hall Square being unveiled, 25 June 1898. At the ceremony were Henry Lane's widow, the 8th Earl De La Warr and Earl Brassey. The houses in the background are to the west of the Town Hall and are now incorporated into the building.

Henry Lane (1827-1895), 1894. Known as 'The Father of Local Government in Bexhill' Henry Lane was the first chairman of the Bexhill Local Board, The Bexhill Urban District Council and the first resident Justice of the Peace for Bexhill. He lived at Broadoak Manor on Broadoak Lane.

The opening of the Town Hall, 27 April 1895. Sir Joseph Renals, Lord Mayor of London, is declaring the Town Hall open, beside him, in uniform, is Viscount Cantelupe who became 8th Earl De La Warr the following year. Sir Joseph and Lady Renals were guests of Viscount and Lady Cantelupe at the Manor House in January 1895, and were persuaded to come back later in the year for the opening. The state coach and horses were brought down from London by train. The Town Hall was actually built in 1894 and the bronze commemorative plaque in the Town Hall was unveiled in July 1895.

The Earl's reception at the Town Hall, 1900. The 8th Earl had gone to South Africa as a war correspondent for *The Globe* and had been injured while attempting to rescue a wounded soldier. The rest of the local troops returned at the end of the Boer War in 1902 and were taken home by motorcar.

Ebenezer Howard, Bexhill's first mayor in 1902. The draft Charter of Incorporation named the 8th Earl De La Warr as provisional mayor, but his divorce during the summer of 1902 turned public opinion against him and a new candidate had to be quickly found. The 8th Earl was however made mayor in 1903.

The reception of the Charter of Incorporation, 21 May 1902. Crowds gather for the reading of the Charter at the Town Hall. In 1902 Bexhill was granted a royal Charter of Incorporation; it was the last Sussex town to be incorporated and this was also the first royal charter granted by Edward VII. Borough status gave Bexhill the right to elect its first mayor. It is believed that this was the first time a royal charter was ever delivered by motorcar.

Ritz cinema, Buckhurst Road, May 1951. The Ritz was built on the site previously occupied by a roller skating rink on Buckhurst Road. It was opened in 1937 and closed in 1961. The telephone exchange was built on the site in 1970.

Ritz cinema Staff, 1951. The Ritz was the last cinema to be built in Bexhill and the grandest. The Kursaal was the first venue in town to show moving pictures in 1898, the Bijou, in Town Hall Square, was the first purpose-built cinema (1910-1954), the others were the Cinema de Luxe, Western Road (1913-1921), The Picture Playhouse, Western Road (1921-present), and The Gaiety, London Road (1935-1940).

Beulah Baptist church, Buckhurst Road, c. 1910. Construction work started on the church in April 1897 and was completed in August 1898. Designed in the fourteenth century gothic style by Mr Resta W. Moore it was built at a cost of £1,000 by Charles Thomas.

Bexhill Convent at the Feast of Corpus Christi, 11 June 1914. 'Our Ladye's Convent' was built in 1914 on Buckhurst Road; the houses in the background are on Upper Sea Road. There have also been a number of small schools on the site, St Joseph's Day School opened in 1917, then The Froebel Preparatory School and Loretto College girls' day school in 1937. Hythe House Preparatory School opened there in 1938, and Little St. Francis Kindergarten in 1948. The Convent was bought in 1946 by the Embankment Fellowship Centre and in September 1946 Lord Hollenden opened it as Hollenden House ex-servicemen' Rest Home. Still called Hollenden House the property is now a residential care home.

Sea Road decorated for the Lord Mayor of London's visit, 21 July 1906. Sir W. Vaughan Morgan came to Bexhill to open the extension to Egerton Park in 1906. The Lord Mayor stayed at the Metropole Hotel. Note the flower seller by the De La Warr Gates, she has very sensibly set up her stall on the public side of the gates and not on the Earl's property.

Clock House, 1888. This is a very early photograph and there are few other buildings in the background. Clock House stands on the junction of Sea Road and Endwell road. Note the rubble in the street; Bexhill-on-Sea would have had the appearance of one large building site at this time.

Bexhill Central Station, c. 1925. Taxis and a bus wait outside ready for passengers. The station, which was opened in 1902, was built on a bridge over the railway line. The billboard on the left is on the blowhole that stopped smoke and steam backing up in the tunnel and blowing back onto the platforms. The blowhole was blocked up and the wall pulled down in 1964.

The Granville Hotel, 1936. Building work started in June 1901 and finished in 1902, however due to a bar licensing problem (the station was fully licensed and the authorities were unwilling to give one to another property so close) it did not open for business until 1905. The Granville was more recently renamed the Grand Hotel.

Sea Road and St Barnabas' church, c. 1898. The church was built in 1890 and completed in 1891; it was designed by Sir Arthur Blomfield. St Barnabas was the new parish church for the resort as St Peter's was not large enough for the sudden increase in parishioners. The independent parish of St Barnabas came into existence on 26 June 1891.

The junction of Sea Road and Cantelupe Road, c. 1904. It is not certain what this occasion is; it may be one of the cars from the 1904 races or simply one of the wealthier residents showing off their new vehicle. St Barnabas' church is in the background.

Sea Road, May 1951. The trolleybus cables are overhead although the tramlines were removed in about 1930. The blowhole for the railway line is on the left with a telephone box at the southern end, behind this is 1 Station Road, Baird Court. This was the home of John Logie Baird (1888-1946) the inventor of the television who moved here in 1941 and remained there until his death in 1946.

Sydenham House, Sea Road, 1936. On the northern corner of Sea Road and Cantelupe Road was Sydenham House, a popular café that was built in 1897. During the Second World War it was used by military personnel based in Bexhill and was known as 'Forces Corner'. Civilians working there were issued with a curfew pass so that the café could stay open into the evening for the troops.

St Mary Magdalene's church, 1926. St Mary's was built in 1907, the former mission hall and clergy house, which opened in 1891, became St Mary Magdalene's Primary School and is now a church hall.

Tram in Sea Road, 17 April 1906. The tram service started in 1906 and ran between St Leonards and the Metropole Hotel, later in the year it was extended to Cooden Beach. It was replaced by a trolleybus service in 1928. On the right is Magdalene Road. Just behind the tram is a coffee van which was provided by Canon Mortlock of St Barnabas' church, to try and keep people out of the pubs; in 1907 it was moved from here to the Sackville Arch.

Devonshire Road with tram, *c.* 1910. Devonshire Road was one of the main shopping streets in Bexhill. The trams came down Magdalene Road, Sea Road, Endwell Road, and Devonshire Road, and then onto Marina until the turnaround that is now the Sackville Road roundabout.

Upper Sea Road, *c.* 1895. This is on the crest of the hill looking from the Old Town, the original Bexhill village, down into the new resort of Bexhill-on-Sea. The junction with Buckhurst Road is on the right.

Building the premises that became Longley Brothers Ltd, Devonshire Road, *c.* 1903. On the left are the *Bexhill Observer* Offices. These buildings were bombed in 1942 and the *Observer* offices relocated to Western Road in 1947 and later to Sackville Road, where it is to this day. After the war Longley's were able to develop the bombsite into an extension for their shop.

Railway station goods yard, *c.* 1910. The railway line opened in 1846 with a small halt to serve Bexhill village. In 1891 a station fronting Devonshire Square was built, the current Central Station opened in 1902. The goods vans are ready to deliver their parcels to shops and homes throughout Bexhill, 'L.B. & S.C.R.' stands for the London Brighton and South Coast Railway. The goods yard was where Sainsbury's car park is today.

Tradesmen's carriages in Station Square, now Devonshire Square, *c*. 1900. One of the delivery vans is Mark Bateup's, who had bakeries in Belle Hill and Salisbury Road. In the background to the left is Bexhill's first telephone exchange, which opened in 1898 with thirty-three subscribers. In the middle is the railway station and to the right is a building that was Bexhill's first railway station, a simple halt that was built when the line opened in 1846. Just visible on the far left is the corner of the Devonshire Hotel.

Devonshire Road from Western Road, *c*. 1900. Viewed from the window of the Riches and Gray offices. The junction with St Leonards Road is on the other side of the road.

Riches and Gray, 1895. The estate agents offices were on the corner of Devonshire Road and Western Road. Here there is a floral arch decoration at the end of Western Road to celebrate the Lord Mayor of London's visit to Bexhill to open the Town Hall in 1895.

Boots staff 1967. The gathering is for the retirement of the Manager Councillor George Woodfine, the elderly gentleman in the middle of the group. He was the manager of the Bexhill branch from 1923-1967. Boots originally only had the property adjacent to the corner of Parkhurst Road; the corner plot was occupied by Mr F. Wimshurst chemists until taken over by Boots.

The Maharajah of Cooch Behar's funeral, 21 September 1911. The funeral cortege is here passing down Devonshire Road towards the railway station. The Maharajah's family had visited Bexhill before, but it was on the advice of his doctors that the Maharajah came to 22 Marina Court Avenue to try and regain his health.

Station Road viewed from the footbridge, 1939. The Central Station and St Mary Magdalene's church are in the distance. The winter of 1939/1940 was very cold and there were heavy snowstorms in Bexhill.

Gala week, Station Road, July 1934. The ornate building on the far side of the road is Caffyns' garage. Caffyns established their garage during the First World War and added this striking frontage in the 1920s. During the 1930s 16 Station Road was the home and shop of Arthur Spray 'The Mysterious Cobbler' who was renown for his healing powers.

Bexhill Horse Parade, Station Road, 1 June 1914. After starting on De La Warr Parade the participants would make their way to the Town Hall for the prize giving. In the background to the left are covered taxi ranks, part of the Central Station. These have since been lost but during the First World War they served as an indoor market. On the right is the station's goods yard; this is now Sainsbury's car park.

Western Road decorated for the Lord Mayor's visit, 1895. A misty, presumably early morning, view of Western Road and the triumphal arch built to welcome the Lord Mayor of London. The men in the photograph built the arch.

Western Road, c. 1910. Note the South East & Chatham Railway Company's van delivering goods that have been brought into town by rail to the Bexhill West Station in Terminus Road.

Western Road Garage, *c.* 1936. The left hand side of the building was originally the Cinema de Luxe, which opened in 1913. It's owners bought the land next to it and built the Picture Playhouse cinema which opened in 1921, at this time the Cinema de Luxe closed. In 1921 the Cinema de Luxe became the Carter and Lidstone garage, the right-hand side of the building was added in 1923 to create the Western Road Garage.

Inside The Western Road Garage, *c.* 1923. This part of the building is now The Mall. The *Bexhill Observer* moved here in 1947 because their offices in Devonshire Road were bombed in 1942. The *Observer* was first published on 9 May 1896 to cover the Duchess of Teck's visit to open the Kursaal. Its main rival was the *Bexhill Chronicle* that began in September 1887 and was eventually incorporated into the *Bexhill Observer* in 1930.

18 Western Road, 1918. Western Road was originally residential, it was only later developed into a shopping area. This photograph shows one of the houses before being converted into a shop. The woman and girl outside are Ethel and Victoria Whiteman.

Sackville Road, 1930. This is an empty plot next to Buck's garage at the southern end of Sackville Road. In the foreground are tram tracks that had been taken up as the trams were replaced by trolleybuses in 1928.

George Brisley's chemist shop, London Road, *c.* 1894. George Brisley had three daughters, Ethel, Joyce and Nina. Joyce and Nina went on to be successful authors and illustrators of children's books, Joyce is best known for her Milly-Molly-Mandy stories which were published from 1928 onwards.

Sanyer's Circus in London Road, *c.* 1899. London Road was originally called Station Road because, before the development of the resort, it was the main route from the railway halt to Belle Hill. It was one of the early shopping centres in Bexhill. The building on the other side of the road is Brisley's chemist shop.

The junction of London Road and Belle Hill, 1962. The bridge carrying the Crowhurst branch line over the road was near here, its shadow can dbe seen in the foreground.

An Elva car, London Road, c. 1955. Bexhill is the birthplace of British motor racing and also the home of Elva cars. Frank Nichols (1920-1997) opened his Elva works in London Road in 1955, the business moved to Rye in 1961 and production ended in 1969.

Bexhill Down, *c.* 1910. St Stephen's church and the Down Mill can be seen on the skyline. St Stephen's was opened in 1900 and was paid for by John Lambert Walker of Woodsgate Park. The windmill was built around 1735 and fell down in 1965.

Clearing up after a blizzard, Bexhill Down, March 1887. This photograph was taken by George Herbert Gray, Earl De La Warr's estate manager. It was recorded that some of these heaps of snow did not completely disappear until the beginning of June.

Old Folks Dinner in Down Drill Hall, February 1912. This event was organized by the Bexhill Buffaloes. Sitting in the foreground is Alderman 'Honest' John Greed.

Badminton in Drill Hall, c. 1928. The town's first drill hall was behind the Queen's Head on Belle Hill; this one was opened by Earl Brassey in 1901.

St Leonards Road, 21 July 1906. Seen here from Sea Road, the street has been decorated for the Lord Mayor of London's visit.

St Leonards Road, 5 June 1911. Carriages taking part in the Bexhill Horse Parade are passing by. St. Leonards Road was the scene of a very serious fire in 1924 at the Miller and Franklin Store, now the site of the Job Centre. Fireman S.A. Wise, nephew of Captain Wise, was killed and a marble tombstone in the likeness of a fireman in action was built for him by public subscription in Bexhill cemetery.

Motorcar parade, St Leonards Road, 1904. A procession around town was a vital ingredient in all of Bexhill's early events; it was no different with the motorcar races of 1902 and 1904. Devonshire Road can be seen in the background.

Sackville Road Methodist church, c. 1896. Seen here nearly completed with the glazing being installed. The church was planned in 1895 and designed by Mr W.W. Pocock, the twelve foundation stones were laid on Easter Monday in 1896 and it was opened that July. Vestries were added in 1924 and a new entrance in 1961. Parkhurst Hall, which was used as a chapel, meeting hall and schoolroom prior to the building of the church, was opened in 1892; one of the foundation stones was laid by Viscountess Cantelupe.

St Georges Road, winter 1910. Near the junction of London Road and St George's Road was a mineral spring. The water was described as 'chalybeate' but rusty might have been a better description. One entrepreneur bottled the water for sale in London.

The Bexhill and District motor bus, Clinch Green, 1926. Seen here near the cemetery gates. The service was run by Carter & Lidstone Ltd and operated out of their garage in Green Lane, Little Common.

Bexhill Gasworks, Ashdown Road, c. 1935. Here coal was brought in by rail and then converted into gas. The gasworks were opened in 1887 and the first gas streetlights were turned on in Bexhill in August 1888. There was a serious fire at the site in 1922. A gas main from London serving this part of Sussex was opened in 1966 and the gasworks were closed in April 1967, and demolished in 1968. It is sometimes confused with the Hastings Gasworks, which curiously were within Bexhill at Glyne Gap, these closed in 1969.

Bexhill West Station, Terminus Road, c. 1907. The Bexhill West Station opened in 1902 as part of the Crowhurst Line. This connected Bexhill and Sidley to the main Hastings to London line and made the journey half an hour quicker than it is today.

The platforms of the Bexhill West Station, *c.* 1905. The station closed in 1964 and the building is now an auction house. The old line up to the Down was turned into a road and renamed Beeching Road, sidings and engine shed areas becoming an industrial estate.

The Crowhurst Viaduct, *c.* 1900. The Crowhurst branch line and its viaduct, the 'Seventeen arches' as it was known locally, was built between January 1898 and 1900. The line opened 31 May 1902 and was closed in 1964; the viaduct was later declared unsafe and blown up in 1969.

Lifeboat Day, 1934. The woman selling the flags is Mrs Fowler. To the left is Terminus Road and in the background is Windsor Road.

Hastings to Bexhill tramway, c. 1925. At Glyne Gap, rather than go along the road, the trams ran through the fields to Bulverhythe.

Four

Parks

The Egerton Park Pergola, c. 1920. Egerton Park was laid out in 1888 and extended in 1906. The Pergola began as an open-air stage in 1906 and had covered sides and dressing rooms added in 1909. In 1932/1933 The Park Pavilion was built on the site, this was a combination of theatre and indoor bowling green. The Bexhill West railway station can just be seen in the distance.

Egerton Park Baths, *c.* 1929. Baths were an original feature of the park from 1889 and were finally demolished in 1987. The open-air pool was filled with unheated seawater. In the background is Bexhill Museum which opened in 1914; it is housed in a park shelter hall that was built in 1903.

Girls from St Christopher's School at the Egerton Park Baths, *c.* 1920. At this time the changing cubicles ran all along the inner walls of the swimming pool. In the early 1960s the facilities were upgraded and a children's pool added at the east end.

The Egerton Park model boating pond, *c.* 1930. This is still a popular feature of the park, although the model boats are now more sophisticated. In the background is the main boating pond.

The rocking horses in Egerton Park, *c.* 1929. These were the main feature of the children's playground in the park since the 1920s. Sadly they were stolen from the park in the 1990s, only one which was away for repair at the time survived, and that is now displayed in the Museum.

Egerton Park floodlit in 1937. In the 1930s there were streetlights and floodlights throughout Egerton Park, allowing it to be used late into the evening. This would have been particularly useful when there were evening performances at the Park Pavilion.

Egerton Park Pavilion, 1936. Here set up for bowls but to the left the theatre stage can be seen. Bowls were played along one axis and the theatre was set up at right angles to it, allowing bowls to be played during the day and shows to be put on in the evening.

Egerton Park Rangers, c. 1920. One of the local football teams in the corner of Egerton Park. Bexhill's first football club was formed in 1889 and played at Belle Hill Farm, where the fire station in London Road now stands. Bexhill Town football club was formed through the amalgamation of the Bexhill and Bexhill United clubs. Bexhill Wanderers was founded in 1937 and after the Second World War formed a new Bexhill Town football club, who in 1948 played a charity match against Arsenal.

The 1936 Open Bowls Tournament, Polegrove. The Bexhill Corporation bought the Polegrove from John Webb in 1912 and used it as a rubbish tip; this raised the land surface by six feet in places and in 1920 was laid out as a recreational ground. The Polegrove was officially opened in May 1923. Bowling greens were made in 1923; the first was upgraded to Cumberland turf in 1925 and the second in 1926. The August Week open tournaments began in 1933, the same year as the founding of Bexhill's first women's bowling club.

Miniature golf, c. 1928. Now the site of Clock Tower Court in Park Avenue, the corner of Bexhill Museum can be seen in the background. The former site of the Metropole Hotel on the seafront is still used for miniature golf.

Cantelupe Gardens, c. 1895. This park was behind Marine Mansions and bisected by a path that later became Knole Road. In the background to the left the Metropolitan Convalescent Home can just be seen. Cantelupe Gardens were developed into croquet lawns by the Bexhill Croquet Club. In 1952 Charles Gulliver opened a bowling green to the east of Knole Road and in 1954 built an indoor bowls pavilion and clubhouse.

Five
The De La Warr Pavilion

The De La Warr Pavilion, 1935. Seen here during the final phases of construction. Note how close to the Metropole the Pavilion is. In the foreground, from left to right, is the Colonnade, the Rowing Club boathouse and 22 Marina Court Avenue, where the Maharajah of Cooch Behar died in 1911.

Some of the workman who built the Pavilion, 1935. The Pavilion was built during the course of 1935 and cost £70,000. The 9th Earl De La Warr specified in the contract that the project should use as much local labour as possible because there was an economic depression.

The plaque laying ceremony at the Pavilion, 6 May 1935. Present were the 9th Earl and Countess De La Warr with their children. The plaque, which is at the bottom of the southern staircase, commemorated the Silver Jubilee of King George V. The King had visited the building site earlier in the year.

The De La Warr Pavilion at night, 1935. Note that there are posters for the inaugural concert on the billboard for 14 December 1935. The three flagpoles in the foreground are no longer there and were complemented by three poplar trees closer to the building.

De La Warr Pavilion entrance hall, c. 1950. The inner set of entrance doors had not yet been added, making the hall larger than it is now. The box office is recessed so as not to obstruct the hall and access to the north stairs is next to it. The theatre foyer is on the left and the café and restaurant on the right.

The De La Warr Pavilion restaurant, 1936. Furnished with Alto chairs and tables. At the far end of the room is the mural by Wadsworth; this now hangs in the entrance hall. One end of the room was a café and the far end was a restaurant.

The De La Warr Pavilion library, 1935. At the back of the sun lounge was the library, although no longer in the Pavilion it was built in keeping with the ethos of self-improvement behind the building. Next to this was the sun parlour, a roofed but unglazed area where people could enjoy the bracing air, this was soon glazed in as the public proved to be less keen on fresh air than was first thought!

The De La Warr Pavilion theatre, 1935. With acoustic tiles on the ceiling and fold away seating the theatre was a massive improvement on the facilities previously available in Bexhill. The theatre has always been the heart of the Pavilion but the building has many other amenities to offer.

Games on the deck of the De La Warr Pavilion, c. 1936. An important element of the original plan for the Pavilion was the use of the roof; it was intended to be used for games as if it were the deck of an ocean liner. In the background is Marina Court.

The Duke and Duchess of York (later King George VI and Queen Mother) opening the De La Warr Pavilion, 12 December 1935. Between the Duke and Duchess are the mayor of Bexhill and the 9th Earl De La Warr, the inspiration behind the De La Warr Pavilion.

The royal visit to Bexhill, 1966. Her Majesty Queen Elizabeth II and the Duke of Edinburgh toured the De La Warr Pavilion in 1966. With them is the mayor of Bexhill, Margaret Ackland. The following day the Queen visited the stricken Welsh village of Aberfan and an appeal arranged by nurses at Bexhill during the Queen's visit raised over £228 for disaster relief.

Six

Fire

Bexhill Fire Brigade, 1922. In the middle of the front row is the chairman of the fire brigade Councillor R.C. Sewell, on the left are Captain F.G. Wise and Mr L. Russell of Russell's Garage who maintained the fire engine, on the right are Captain F.S. Dunn, the former chairman, and Lieutenant A.J. Stevens who succeeded Captain Wise in 1925. Bexhill's first fire brigade started in 1888. This fire station was in Amherst Road, behind the Town Hall, from 1896 until 1971.

FIRE AT BEXHILL-ON-SEA, NOV 3RD 1909.   VIELER, PHOTO, BEXHILL.

Endwell Road fire, 3 November 1909. A very serious fire at a house called 'Arden' at the corner of Endwell Road and Wilton Road. The fire started at 11 a.m. and the alarm was raised by Miss Church who lived there with the invalid Mrs Smith and Miss Smith, all of whom were safely rescued.

Devonshire Road fire, 10 October 1912. Fires always seemed to draw a huge crowd; here are some of the younger residents posing for the photograph.

Fire at the Sackville Hotel, 1912. Next to the Sackville Hotel was The Salisbury Hotel; shortly after the date of this picture the building became Links House and then The Bexe, both private hotels.

Motor fire engine *Helena, c.* 1922. This is the naming ceremony outside the Town Hall.

Naming ceremony of the fire engine *Diana*, 7 March 1925. Named after the Countess De La Warr who is at the wheel of the fire engine with her husband the 9th Earl. The Town Hall is in the background. After a tour round Bexhill, Countess De La Warr drove the fire engine back to the Town Hall.

Naming of the Motor fire engine *Lady Kitty* at the Town Hall, 1931. Lady Kitty is the daughter of the 9th Earl De La Warr, seen here with Captain Jim Stevens with whom she made friends. When she was asked to present a bouquet to the Duchess of York at the opening of the De La Warr Pavilion she would only agree if Captain Stevens came with her.

Seven
Schools

St Barnabas School, Western Road, Infants class 1927-28. The school opened in 1893 on the corner of Western Road and Sackville Road. The school served the parish of Barnabas and was mixed until 1898, after this the infants were educated on the ground floor and the girls upstairs. The school closed during the Second World War and in 1951 the building became the town library.

St Barnabas Boys' School, Reginald Road, 1927-28. The boy's school opened in 1898 in Reginald Road and the Western Road school continued as an infant and girls' school. The school closed in 1956 when St Peter's and St Paul's School opened in Buckhurst Road. The building and its above ground air raid shelter still survives.

The Down School, c. 1910. The Down School, or Bexhill Council School as titled here, is now King Offa School; it was opened in 1907 and extended in 1912. The school was built close to the drill hall on Bexhill Down. The infant school is now just below this building and the High School just above it.

Pupils at the Down School, 1924. Bexhill High School was built just to the north of the Down School and opened in 1943, it became co-educational in 1965 and was then called the Down Secondary Modern School.

Teachers at the Down School, c. 1938. Taken a year or two before the disruption caused by the Second World War and the evacuation of Bexhill's schools. The Down can be seen in the background.

All Saints Infant School, Sidley, 1910. The school opened in 1865 and was enlarged in 1910. By special dispensation the school was also a place of worship until the Iron church was built in 1885.

The County Secondary School, Sidley, c. 1934. The Boys Grammar School and the Girls Grammar School were built next to each other but were strictly segregated. The grammar schools opened in 1926 and had a formal opening by the Duchess of Atholl in 1927. The schools were amalgamated in 1970 and are now Bexhill College.

Infants from St Mark's Church of England School, Little Common, 1904. St Mark's School was opened in 1855, enlarged in 1863 and again in 1890. The school was closed in 1961 and the building demolished in 1967.

St Leonard's School, Woodsgate, c. 1905. One of Bexhill's many independent schools. There have been over 300 schools in Bexhill, however many of these were quite small and did not always survive for very long. The St Leonard's School was at the former home of John Lambert Walker of Woodsgate Park and opened shortly after his death in 1903.

St Hilary's School for Girls, Bexhill, *c.* 1912. Founded in 1901 by Misses Hall and Johnson in Hastings Road the school moved to De La Warr Road until finally going to Normanhurst Court, Catsfield, in the early 1920s. This was the former residence of the Brassey family.

Colwall Court, *c.* 1936. The School of Domestic Economy opened in 1935 and operated until July 1958. In June 1959 the building became a holiday home for the Stars Organisation for Spastics and it is now Phoenix House.

Eight

War

The 2nd Cinque Ports Artillery Volunteers, Drill Hall, c. 1890. This drill hall was behind the Queen's Head on Belle Hill and was built in 1887. The first drill hall on the Down, near King Offa School, was built in 1901 and opened in December that year by Earl Brassey. A second drill hall was built on its west side for the local Territorials in 1914 and opened in January 1915.

Bexhill Battery preparing guns on the Down, 1914. Here the local troops are mobilising at the start of the First World War.

Tents at Cooden Camp, c. 1914. Cooden Camp was set up in the grounds of Henry Young's property of Cooden Mount; here Lieutenant Colonel Claude Lowther of Herstmonceux raised 'Lowther's Lambs', the 11th, 12th and 13th Battalions of the Royal Sussex Regiment.

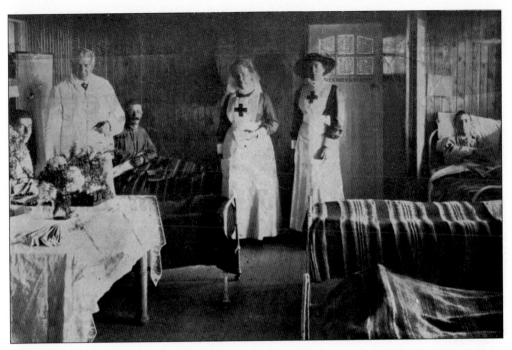

Cooden Camp Hospital, 1914. Another military hospital was established in Bexhill in Cantelupe Road.

The Army Hut, Cooden Camp, c. 1914. Soldiers relaxing off duty, at the back of the room are some of the nurses from No. 38 Voluntary Aid Detachment.

Reading the war bulletins at the Colonnade, 1914.

Bexhill Tradesmen's Stretcher Bearers Company, 1914. The building in the background is Marine Crescent on West Parade.

The 8th Earl De La Warr commanding the motor cruiser *Nord Est*, 1914. Just before the war began the Earl had been divorced for a second time and was being pursued through the courts by his creditors. This is the last known photograph of the Earl who contracted fever while returning from leave in 1915 and died in Messina.

Peace thanksgiving service, 6 July 1919. The service was held at the Egerton Park Pergola. Although the armistice was in 1918 the war did not officially end until 1919.

Peace Day procession in Sackville Road, 19 July 1919. The declaration of peace was read out at the Town Hall on 2 July 1919, and a thanksgiving service was held at the Park Pergola on 6 July 1919.

The Creek Road School, Deptford, on Bexhill Down, 1939. This was one of the London schools evacuated to Bexhill at the start of the Second World War. Blackheath and Kidbrooke boys' school, All Saints girls from Blackheath and Roan girls school, Greenwich, also came to Bexhill. There were 540 juniors in total and another 178 secondary school pupils from St Joseph's Academy, Blackheath. With the fall of France in June 1940 the south coast was suddenly vulnerable and all pupils were evacuated.

Demobilised Men's Day, 10 September 1919. The service for the men who had just returned home after the war was held at the Colonnade.

Filling sandbags from the beach, September 1939. Staff from the De La Warr Pavilion, with some younger helpers, are building air raid defences around the Colonnade. The corner of the Metropole Hotel is in the background.

The Colonnade protected by sandbags, September 1939. The Metropole Hotel and De La Warr Pavilion both suffered bomb damage during the war. There were fifty-one air raids on Bexhill and twenty-two people were killed.

An air raid shelter being built in Short Lane, off Chantry Lane, September 1939. One of the brick walls of this shelter still survives against the bank. Another air raid shelter is still built into the bank half way up Upper Sea Road.

The Playhouse cinema, Western Road, 1939. The cinema reopened in September 1939, note the gasmask cases carried by the people in the queue. The Playhouse, now the Curzon Picture Playhouse, opened in 1921 and is Bexhill's only surviving cinema.

Helpers at the Park Pavilion canteen, 1939. This was the Egerton Park Theatre which, like the Museum building, was commandeered during the war.

ARP headquarters, 1939. The ARP helped to save many lives in Bexhill during the bombing. Most of the damage was caused during 'tip and run' raids in 1942 and V1 'doodle-bug' strikes in 1944.

Schoolgirls being evacuated from Bexhill, July 1940. The boys Grammar School and St Peter's School went to St Albans, the girls Grammar School and Down mixed and Infants, St Barnabas boys and girls, St Peter's boys, St Mark's and St Mary Magdalene's school went to Letchworth. St Peter's infants and Sidley infants went to Stevenage.

The evacuation of schoolchildren, July 1940. The mayor and mayoress, Councillor and Mrs Hughes, are saying goodbye to some of the children being evacuated on Bexhill Central Station. Miss Burrows is in the background. In all 1,120 children left Bexhill in two trainloads. However by the end of 1940 about 350 children, unable to endure being away from home returned. This prompted the reopening of St Barnabas boys, All Saints and St Mark's in January 1941.

Bomb damage to buildings in Devonshire Road, December 1940. Three people were killed. Many buildings in Bexhill were lost due to bombing. Some 328 high explosive bombs and over a thousand incendiaries were dropped on the town. There were also machine gun attacks by fighters and some V1 strikes towards the end of the war.

American aircrew being rescued from a bomber that ditched off Bexhill in 1943. Metal from wrecked aircraft is frequently found on Bexhill beach.

VE Day party on Bexhill Down, 8 May 1945. Jack W. Fowler's Punch and Judy show entertains the children. Uncle Jack's performances were a popular attraction and he would often appear at the Colonnade.

Nine
Sidley, Cooden and Little Common

Sidley Village, 1896. In 1828 this was the site of the famous Battle of Sidley Green where a pitched battle took place between smugglers and customs men. The New Inn, like the Bell, the Queen's Head and the Wheatsheaf, was one of the old coaching inns. In the middle of the eighteenth century the New Inn was known as The Five Bells.

A hunt meeting outside the New Inn, Sidley, c. 1930. A reminder that even up to the start of the Second World War Sidley was still a small rural village set amongst fields. Post-war development filled the farmland with housing estates and joined Sidley to the rest of Bexhill.

The Sussex Hotel, Sidley, c. 1930. The Sussex Hotel replaced the earlier Sussex Inn in 1902. The Sussex Hotel was designed by Henry Ward, who also designed Bexhill Town Hall and St Stephen's church. On the left is F.L. Dobson's grocers shop.

All Saints church Sidley, *c.* 1930. The church was proposed in 1921 but only the nave was completed by 1925, work on the tower began in 1928 and it was consecrated in 1930. It replaced the Iron church, also called All Saints, which was built in 1885. The Iron church was dismantled and rebuilt as part of Beals of Sidley Ltd.

A baby show at All Saints church hall, Sidley, 1941.

Sidley Railway Station, *c.* 1964. The station was opened in 1902 to take advantage of the Crowhurst Branch Line; the Pelham Hotel opposite was also opened at this time. The station building ceased to be used during the Second World War and tickets were then purchased on the platforms. The Line closed in 1964 and the building was used as Sidley Service Station until it was demolished in 1970.

The Pelham Hotel and Sidley Station, *c.* 1910. On the left is the Pelham Hotel; this was built in 1902 by J.P. Goodwin, who also built the York Hall, to coincide with the opening of Sidley railway station, seen here on the right. The photograph is taken from the railway bridge.

Sidley, *c.* 1920. This is the view from the window of Smith & Humphrey's garage at the northern end of Sidley High Street. Note the petrol pump in the foreground.

Lewes Lass Cottages, Sidley, *c.* 1900. The curious cottages were in part built from the timbers of the 183 ton brig *Lewes Lass* which was wrecked off Bexhill on 31 October 1885. The figurehead can be seen on the roof between the two cottages.

Sidley Scout troop, 1927. The first boy scout troop in Bexhill was the 1st Kangaroo Patrol that was formed in 1908; girl guides were established here in 1912.

The Sidley Bowls Club, *c.* 1932. The club was formed during the First World War and originally played on a green that is now the site of the car park. In 1952 the club started playing at the recreation ground on Buxton Drive.

122

Bill Robert at Cooden Mount, *c.* 1895. Cooden Mount was the residence of Henry Young (1842-1929) who owned an iron foundry in Pimlico. Cooden Mount was built at the end of the nineteenth century and was demolished in 1986. During the First World War Henry Young allowed his land to be used by the military as Cooden Camp.

Farming on Cooden Down, *c.* 1900. Brothers Jack and Albert Freeman are pitching and loading, Harry Rhodes is using the long rake and Douglas Young, dressed in white, is in the middle of the picture. The photograph was probably taken by Douglas' brother Gordon; they were the sons of Henry Young of Cooden Mount.

The Coastguard Cottages, Cooden Beach, *c.* 1900. These cottages used to stand opposite what is now the Cooden Beach Hotel, which opened in 1931. The photograph is taken from the railway embankment. Cooden Beach station opened in 1905 as a motor train halt and the present station building opened in 1936.

The Denbigh Hotel, *c.* 1904. Formerly called the Denbigh Arms its name was changed to the Denbigh Hotel in 1900. The hotel is on a rise between Bexhill Old Town and Little Common village.

Little Common Village, 1897. In the late eighteenth and early nineteenth century this was the base of The Little Common Gang of smugglers. The Wheatsheaf Inn, shown on the right of the drawing, is one of the original coaching inns and was substantially modified in 1886.

Blacksmiths and the Wheatsheaf, Little Common, c. 1927. The forge (covered with ivy) is on the left, then Forge House, and the Wheatsheaf Inn is on the right.

Coronation festivities at Little Common, 22 June 1911. Celebrations for the coronation of King George V. The bell-cote of St Mark's church can just be seen on the left.

Children at the Little Folks Home, Little Common, c. 1913. Little Folks Home was a children's home that opened in Little Common in 1911. An extension was later added that was opened by the Duke of York, later King George VI, in October 1930.

Little Common Bonfire Society, 8 November 1947. Bonfire societies played an important part in the community life of all local villages.

Little Common, c. 1926. Today the roundabout is larger and much busier. The war memorial was unveiled on 21 November 1920.

An autogyro at Sir Alan Cobham's Flying Circus, Little Common 1933. This was the first time an autogyro had been seen in the area. The twenty-seater airliner, *Youth of Australia* flew passengers around Bexhill, the 9th Earl De La Warr, Baron Buckhurst and Lady Kitty were some of those to take advantage of this novel experience.

Pear Tree Lane, c. 1930. In September 1937 the first demonstration of television in Bexhill took place at the home of Norman Blackburne in Pear Tree Lane.